Are you on the right path?  awesome? How can you enjo days more fully?

A really great question can change your life. Join us on a Mind Hike, a journey to help you illuminate your life path and make the right choices for you.

Mind Hike is a series of 365 targeted questions in a journal format for everybody. This is a two-way journey. After you complete the initial questions, you will revisit each one a second time to see how you and your life have changed over time. Your Mind Hike journey will get you thinking about what is important to you, what is working in your life, and ultimately, what will bring you joy, success and satisfaction.

This guided Mind Hike journey will help you:
*   Be intentional about the choices that you make.
*   Be clear about your goals and your priorities.
*   Think through your relationships and how (or if) to move forward.
*   Develop a plan for the future.

Embark with us on Mind Hike to plumb the depths of your mind and find the answers that are hidden deep inside. Make your life's journey intentional and full of joy. Let Mind Hike be the guide.

Legal Stuff

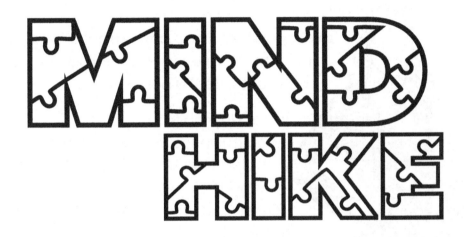

A 365 question journey of self-discovery

PERSONAL EDITION

ABOUT US

ELISSA:

Elissa's grandpa always swore that "Safer" (Elissa's maiden name) meant "horse thief", and that Elissa came from a long line of horse thieves. However, Elissa has yet to steal a horse.

In her day job (as a franchise and business lawyer), Elissa has helped hundreds of people start their own businesses. Outside of work, Elissa swam with sharks in the South Pacific, hiked from border to border in Israel, backpacked through mainland China and is always up for a new adventure.

In recent years, Elissa's adventures have taken a quieter and more harrowing turn-Elissa has become a mom and has also turned her journey inward. Elissa has become an enthusiastic (and unskilled) meditator and an aficionado of anything that has "personal growth" in the title.

MIKE

Dad. Husband. Lawyer. Entrepreneur.
Beer drinker. Look, there's a squirrel.

Welcome to Mind Hike

WHAT IS A MIND HIKE? (DICTIONARY VERSION)

MIND: the element of a person that enables them to be aware of the world and their experiences, to think, and to feel; the faculty of consciousness and thought.

HIKE: to walk or march a great distance, especially through rural areas, for pleasure, exercise, military training, or the like.

WHAT IS A MIND HIKE?
(OUR VERSION)

For the past few years, we have been on
our own journey of self-improvement through
journaling, reading and meditation. We wrote
this journal in the middle of a global pandemic.
We each have adventures we wish we could
embark on. Elissa had hoped to spend time
exploring the world. Mike had plans to visit as
many beer festivals as possible (or at the very
least to spend a few days outside of Colorado).
These big plans didn't turn out so well. So, we
turned to explorations within our own selves.
And Mind Hike (Mike's baby) was born.

Mind Hike, therefore, (we promise this is
the only legalese in this book) for us is a
personal odyssey. It is a time and place for
self-exploration, self-understanding and
self-improvement. We hope that you enjoy
taking the mind hike as much as we have
creating it.

Why Questions?

We've all heard the same phrase for years: "There is no such thing as a stupid question." And some of you may have also heard the related: "Of course there are stupid questions.... And your question was a really stupid question." OK, I may have actually heard that second phrase from my boss (co-author), Mike (Hi, Mike).

While this age-long debate will continue, we believe that a really great question can change your life. (We can't help it, we're both lawyers.) We want to help you illuminate your choices and your path. We hope you enjoy your journey!

How to use this book

 Spend as much or as little time as you want.

 Do a question a day. 2 a day. 45 a day. Whatever. It's your hike; so your pace.

 Make sure to make this a round-trip journey and answer each question at two separate times. It's important to see how your answers and your day-to-day experiences change over time.

 We had originally imagined this journey as a day-by-day exploration (like a daily multi-year journal). But we realized that these questions really should be your own. Do you have a free afternoon? You could complete the first leg of the journey all in one day. Do you feel like answering 10 questions in one sitting? Go for it. Are you on vacation? Responding to the Mind Hike questions would be a great weekend activity.

MIND HIKE

FAQ

(we've tried to answer a few
of your non-stupid questions)

MIND HIKE

? <u>Do I need to start my journal on a certain day?</u> [We already answered this. Read the intro.]

? <u>Do I need to complete one question each day?</u> [Same here. See above.]

? <u>Can I use one word answers?</u> Yes. (See what we did there?) As you can see in our samples, Mike tends to answer quickly in one word answers and Elissa prefers to pontificate (much to her children's dismay). Answer in whatever way is helpful for you.

? <u>What if the questions don't apply for/to me?</u> We're sure you've all played the fortune-cookie game (i.e., add "with a partner" to the end of each fortune — haha, endless amusement). Add or change these questions in any way that is helpful to you, in the same manner.

? <u>What if I don't have an answer?</u> We think not having an answer is actually very instructive. If you don't have an answer, (especially on both rounds of answering) spend some time thinking about why you didn't have an answer. Is it just a question that is irrelevant to you? Or is it an area that you don't think about enough? Is it something you avoid thinking about?

MIND HIKE

? <u>How many questions are there really?</u> 365 if you do it once, 730 if you do it twice. And more if you do bonus questions (we didn't feel like doing the math for the bonus questions but more than 730 for sure). The arrow pointing to the right is for the first round of answers. The arrow pointing to the left is for the second go around.

? <u>What should I do with my answers?</u> Our favorite part of these inner journeys is actually trying to get out of our own heads (occupational hazard for anyone who spends a lot of time by themselves at their computer). We like to think about it as blunt honesty: you peer inside, scoop it out, and then look at it all with clear eyes. "It" being all those dreams and all the angst that we all have clogging up our brains. Once you have it all out in the open, you may want to handle the next steps alone. Or you may want to enlist a friend. We urge you to look for patterns and "a-ha" moments. Has anything changed in your second go-around with the questions? What have you been focusing on? What is holding you back? (Ah, an answer with more questions.)
Finally, we encourage you to join us on our Mind Hike blog (www.mindhikejourney.com) and join other adventurers who are also on this journey. We hope we can all provide guidance and support for each other.

? <u>What should I do in the Free Space?</u> You can do anything you want with the Free Space space. Hence the name, Free Space. (Darn. We used legalese again. Sorry about that.) You can list gratitude points, draw doodles, further elaborate on the question... seriously. Anything you want. In our ideal world, you will have a life-changing epiphany that you might write down (inspired of course, by a brilliant

question you've just answered). But you can use it to jot down your grocery list or just doodle, if that's your preference.

? <u>Tell me about the Bonus Questions.</u> This is not even a question. #FAQFAIL. The bonus questions are additional questions (bonus) that go deeper into a topic or take a question in a different direction. Feel free to answer them, ignore them or turn them into Free Space (see Free Space FAQ above).

? <u>What's all this about a round-trip journey?</u> Glad you asked! We all want to go somewhere, but we've got to return home eventually. The idea behind Mind Hike is to take your journey by answering 365 questions, and revisiting those same questions to figure out what you've learned on your travels.

MIND HIKE

MIKE'S SAMPLE

 What was your most
recent great idea?

⇒ Write a book.   Date 10/1/20
(bucket list item)
(fun experience)
(learn process)

⇐ Write a sequel   Date 10/1/21
to the book
(continue above points)
(fun)

Free Space
Ideas
write follow up book
start blog

To Do: Fix Computer issue

MIND HIKE

ELISSA'S SAMPLE

To do list

What item has been on your to-do list the longest?

Date 3/18/19

Reviewing resumes and responding to job candidates. Yuck

Date 8/5/19

Responding to those job candidates! Just kidding. Choosing a college counselor for Sam :)

Free Space ooh. Deep thought (although probably obvious to anyone else). I'm avoiding any task that I feel emotional about. Like - deciding to hire someone now or next year. And sending my baby to college :)

MIND HIKE

ACKNOWLEDGEMENTS

Mike

I would like to thank Brenda, Eli, Emma and Pierce (Jackson). You make life fun. I would also like to thank my baby sister Tracy Weldon for supporting me and inspiring me to be a better person. I would also like to thank Jeffrey Stuffings. You are the best book club member a person could ask for. And finally, Mom. Thanks for always saying that I am your favorite (even though we know Tracy is).

Elissa

I dedicate this book to all my favorite people in the world: Steve, Sam, Lily, my parents, my favorite brother and the friends that share my days. You make everything better.

WELCOME
TO YOUR JOURNEY

QUESTION 1

Are you happy?

→   Date
_____

_____

_____

_____

←   Date

Free Space

MIND HIKE

QUESTION 2

What keeps you awake at night?

Date

Date

Free Space

MIND HIKE

QUESTION 3

How do you define success?

Date

_____

_____

_____

_____

Date

Free Space

MIND HIKE

QUESTION 4

What is your highest and best purpose?

→ Date
_____

_____

_____

_____

_____

← Date

Free Space

MIND HIKE

QUESTION 5

Who is your biggest champion (in your family)?

Date
_____

_____

_____

_____

Date

Bonus Question: Outside of your family?

What is your best hidden skill?

Date
_____

_____

_____

_____

_____

Date

Bonus Question: How often do you use this skill?

MIND HIKE

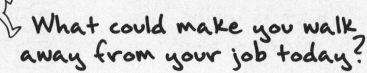

QUESTION 7

What could make you walk away from your job today?

Date
_____

_____

_____

_____

Date

Free Space

MIND HIKE

QUESTION 8

When was the last time you crossed the line?

Date
_____

Date
_____

Free Space

MIND HIKE

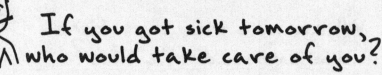

QUESTION 9

If you got sick tomorrow, who would take care of you?

Date
_____

_____

_____

_____

_____

Date

Free Space

MIND HIKE

QUESTION 10

What was the best year of your life?

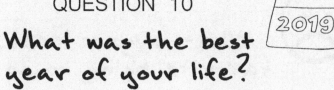

Date
_____

_____

_____

_____

_____

Date

Bonus Question: **The worst year?**

MIND HIKE

QUESTION 11

What is your least favorite thing to do?

Date
_____

_____

_____

_____

Date

Bonus Question: **Favorite?**

QUESTION 12

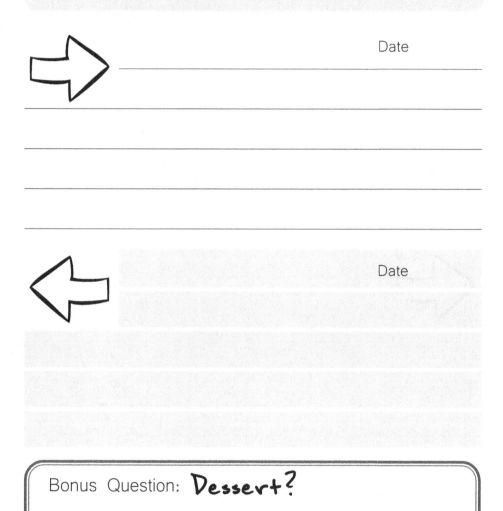

If you were a food, what food would you be?

Date
_____

Date

Bonus Question: **Dessert?**

MIND HIKE

QUESTION 13

Are you more liked in your family or at your job?

Date
_____

Date

Free Space

MIND HIKE

QUESTION 14

If you had to unfriend one person, who would it be?

Date

Date

Free Space

MIND HIKE

QUESTION 15

What was your most recent great idea?

Date
_____

_____

_____

_____

Date

Free Space

QUESTION 16

What is the most demeaning part of your day?

→ Date
_____

_____

_____

_____

← Date

Bonus Question: **Rewarding?**

MIND HIKE

QUESTION 17

What item has been on your to-do list the longest?

Date
_____

_____

_____

_____

Date

Free Space

MIND HIKE

QUESTION 18

"Absence makes the heart grow fonder." What absence has made your heart grow?

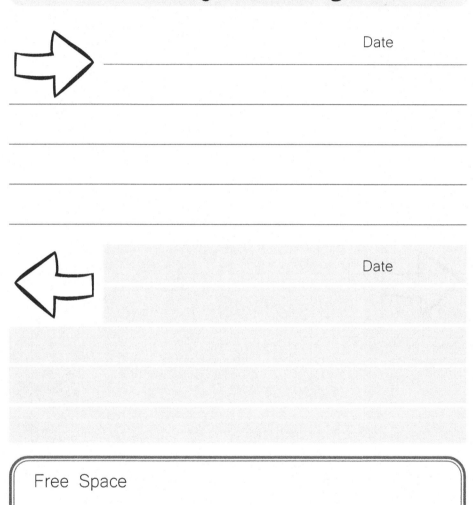

Date
_____

Date

Free Space

MIND HIKE

QUESTION 19

What does your closet look like right now?

Date
_____

_____

_____

_____

_____

Date

Free Space

QUESTION 20

What is the last thing you saved up to buy?

→ _____ Date

_____

_____

_____

← _____ Date

Free Space

MIND HIKE

QUESTION 21

Behind every great person is
_____ (fill in the blank)

Date

Date

Free Space

MIND HIKE

QUESTION 22

If you were granted one wish, what would it be?
(You can't wish for more wishes)

Date
_____

Date

Bonus Question: **2 wishes?**

MIND HIKE

QUESTION 23

What was the last thing you bought that got you in trouble?

Date

Date

Free Space

MIND HIKE

QUESTION 24

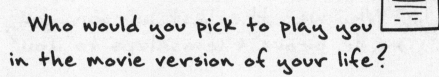

Who would you pick to play you in the movie version of your life?

Date
_____

_____

_____

_____

Date

Free Space

QUESTION 25

Who was the last person you made prove themselves to you?

➡️ _____

Date _____

_____

_____

_____

_____

⬅️

Date _____

Bonus Question: **Why?**

MIND HIKE

What is your go-to drink?

Date

Date

Free Space

MIND HIKE

QUESTION 27

"Keep It Simple, Stupid." How much do you agree or disagree with this?

Date
_____

_____

_____

_____

_____

Date
_____

_____

_____

_____

Free Space

MIND HIKE

QUESTION 28

What characteristic do you look for in a friend?

Date
_____

Date

Bonus Question: **Which friend doesn't have it?**

WWW

What was the last thing you cleared from your search history?

Date
_____

_____
_____
_____
_____

Date

Free Space

MIND HIKE

QUESTION 30

If you could trade places with one
person and live their life,
who would you choose?

Date

Date

Free Space

MIND HIKE

QUESTION 31

Who thinks you are the bad guy?

Date
_____

_____

_____

_____

Date

Free Space

MIND HIKE

QUESTION 32

What is the best compliment you've recently received?

Date
_____

_____

_____

_____

Date

Bonus Question: **Recently given?**

MIND HIKE

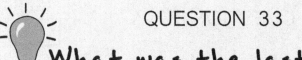

QUESTION 33

What was the last thing you were curious about?

Date
_____

_____

_____

_____

Date

Free Space

MIND HIKE

QUESTION 34

You just found out that you are losing your job next week. What do you do first?

Date
_____

Date

Free Space

1

QUESTION 35

Describe yourself in one word.

Date

Date

Free Space

MIND HIKE

QUESTION 36

"Can't see the forest for the trees." How have you focused on the forest?

Date
_____

_____

_____

_____

Date

Bonus Question: **The trees?**

QUESTION 37

Who is your closest neighbor?

Date
_____

_____

_____

_____

Date

Free Space

QUESTION 38

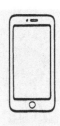

What technology do you hate the most?

➡️

Date
_____

_____

_____

_____

⬅️

Date

Bonus Question: **Like the most?**

QUESTION 39

At what age did you realize you weren't invincible?

→

Date
_____

_____

_____

_____

←

Date

Free Space

MIND HIKE

How connected are you to your community?

→ Date

_____

_____

_____

_____

_____

← Date

Bonus Question: What is your community?

MIND HIKE

QUESTION 41

"Hope for the best and plan for the worst." When was the last time you followed this advice?

Date

Date

Free Space

MIND HIKE

QUESTION 42

What are the biggest threats to your health?

→ Date
_____

_____

_____

_____

← Date

Free Space

MIND HIKE

QUESTION 43

How would your life change today if you inherited a large fortune?

Date

Date

Free Space

MIND HIKE

QUESTION 44 ☆☆☆☆☆

What is your reputation?

➡️ Date
_____

_____

_____

_____

⬅️ Date

Free Space

MIND HIKE

QUESTION 45

What is your most recent success story?

→ Date
_____

_____

_____

_____

_____

← Date

Bonus Question: **Failure?**

MIND HIKE

QUESTION 46

What is your current retirement plan?

Date
_____

Date

Free Space

MIND HIKE

QUESTION 47

If you died today,
who would read the eulogy
at your funeral?

Date
_____

_____

_____

_____

_____

Date

Free Space

MIND HIKE

QUESTION 48

Where would you move if
you could move anywhere?

→ Date
_____

_____

_____

_____

← Date

Free Space

MIND HIKE

QUESTION 49

What is your biggest strength?

Date
_____

_____

_____

_____

Date

Bonus Question: Your second biggest strength?

MIND HIKE

QUESTION 50

What is your go-to song to get you pumped up?

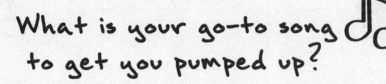

Date

Date

Free Space

MIND HIKE

Guidepost 1

The hardest part of the journey is taking the first step.

GUIDEPOST #1: Well, here you are. You made it this far. Take a load off. There are beers (or water, if that's more your style) on the table.

If you have reached this point, we can only assume that you have made it through this first leg of your journey. Or you've skipped over all of the first set of questions, and landed here anyhow (which is also fine, this is your journey). In either event, welcome! We're happy to see you.

Let's celebrate your ascent through this first part of the journey. Go find someone among your people and spend an hour together. You can be moving or eating or even zooming. Just spend this time together.

TASK: Share 5 questions from your Mind Hike journey with a friend, colleague, mentor or a stranger. Then chat about the questions, the answers and life.

QUESTION 51

Do you trust yourself?

Date
_____

_____

_____

_____

Date

Free Space

MIND HIKE

QUESTION 52

$ When was the last time you looked at your credit card statement?

Date
_____

Date

Free Space

MIND HIKE

QUESTION 53

If someone paid you \$1,000 a day to give up your cell phone, how many days could you do it?

Date
_____

_____

_____

_____

Date

Free Space

MIND HIKE

QUESTION 54

When was the last time you really flew off the handle?

Date
_____

_____

_____

_____

Date

Free Space

MIND HIKE

QUESTION 55

When was the last time you were willing to change?

Date
_____

Date

Bonus Question: **Unwilling?**

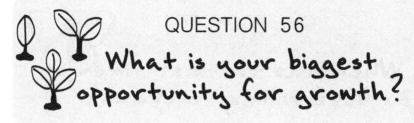

QUESTION 56
What is your biggest opportunity for growth?

Date
_____

_____

_____

_____

Date

Free Space

MIND HIKE

QUESTION 57

When was the last time you blamed someone for something they didn't do?

Date
_____

_____

_____

_____

Date

Bonus Question: **Why?**

MIND HIKE

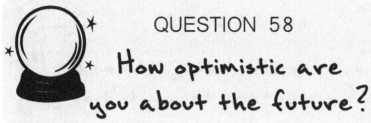

QUESTION 58

How optimistic are you about the future?

Date

Date

Free Space

MIND HIKE

QUESTION 59

When was the last time you were criticized?

→ _____ Date

_____

_____

_____

_____

← _____ Date

_____

_____

_____

_____

Bonus Question: You criticized someone else?

MIND HIKE

QUESTION 60

How has your life not turned out the way you thought it would?

→ Date
_____

_____

_____

_____

← Date

Free Space

QUESTION 61

When was the last time you appreciated your body?

Date

→

←

Date

Free Space

QUESTION 62

What was the last party you attended?

Date
_____

_____

_____

_____

Date

Bonus Question: Did you have fun?

MIND HIKE

QUESTION 63

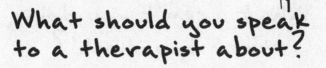

What should you speak to a therapist about?

→

Date
_____

_____

_____

_____

←

Date

Free Space

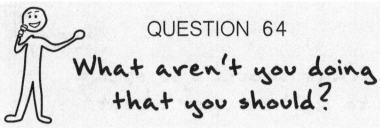

QUESTION 64

What aren't you doing that you should?

→ Date
_____

_____

_____

_____

_____

← Date

Free Space

MIND HIKE

QUESTION 65

Do you spend the right amount of time working?

→ _____ Date

_____

_____

_____

_____

← _____ Date

Bonus Question: How would your family (or friends) answer this question?

QUESTION 66

Where was your last flight to?

Date
_____

_____

_____

_____

Date

Free Space

MIND HIKE

QUESTION 67

When was the last time you
ended a relationship?

➡️ Date
_____

⬅️ Date

Bonus Question: **Why?**

MIND HIKE

QUESTION 68

♫ What was the last concert you went to?

→ _____ Date
_____
_____
_____
_____

← _____ Date

Bonus Question: Who went with you?

MIND HIKE

QUESTION 69

What was your biggest challenge today?

Date

Date

Free Space

MIND HIKE

What was the most productive
thing you've done recently?

Date
_____

_____

_____

_____

_____

Date

Free Space

MIND HIKE

QUESTION 71

Who needs a hug the most?

➡   Date
_____

_____

_____

_____

⬅   Date

Free Space

QUESTION 72

Are you true
to yourself?

Date

Date

Free Space

MIND HIKE

QUESTION 73

What do your friends like best about you?

Date
_____

_____

_____

_____

_____

Date
_____

_____

_____

_____

Bonus Question: **Dislike?**

MIND HIKE

QUESTION 74

In what other job could you be successful?

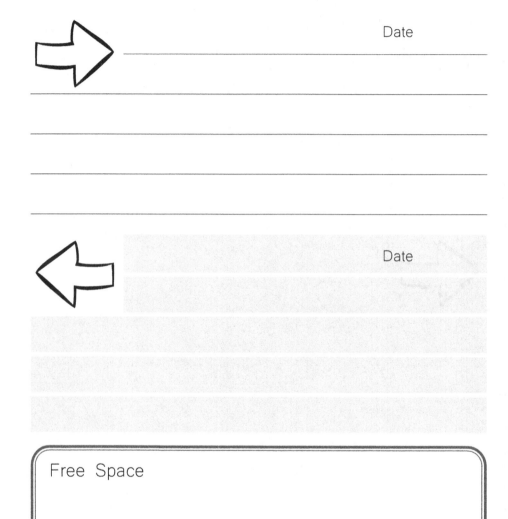

Date
_____

Date

Free Space

MIND HIKE

QUESTION 75

Who is your secret crush?

Date
_____

_____

_____

_____

_____

Date

Free Space

MIND HIKE

QUESTION 76

When was the last time you were stabbed in the front?

Date

Date

"True friends stab you
in the front." - Oscar Wilde

MIND HIKE

QUESTION 77

Who is your favorite person today?

→
Date
_____

_____

_____

_____

←
Date

Free Space

QUESTION 78

What is your biggest distraction?

→ Date
_____

_____

_____

_____

← Date

Free Space

MIND HIKE

QUESTION 79
Who was the last person to annoy you?

Date

_____

_____

_____

_____

Date

Bonus Question: **To make you smile?**

MIND HIKE

QUESTION 80

What do you collect?

Date
_____

_____

_____

_____

Date
_____

_____

_____

_____

Free Space

MIND HIKE

QUESTION 81

What is one thing you can do to improve your mood?

Date

Date

Free Space

MIND HIKE

QUESTION 82

How are you different today than you were one year ago?

Date
_____

Date

QUESTION 83

How well are you paid?

(Or appreciated, if you aren't getting paid?)

Date
_____

_____

_____

_____

Date

Free Space

MIND HIKE

QUESTION 84

What 21st-century skills are you lacking?

Date
_____

_____

_____

_____

Date

Free Space

MIND HIKE

QUESTION 85

What was the last romantic thing that you did?

Date

_____

_____

_____

_____

Date

Free Space

MIND HIKE

QUESTION 86

You are colonizing a new planet and can only bring one person. Who do you bring?

Date

Date

Free Space

MIND HIKE

QUESTION 87

What was the last stupid thing you did?

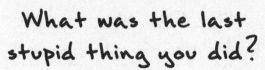

Date
_____

_____

_____

_____

Date

Bonus Question: **Smart thing?**

MIND HIKE

QUESTION 88

What is the most difficult part of your life?

Date
_____

_____

_____

_____

Date

Bonus Question: **Easiest part?**

QUESTION 89

"Thank you for being a friend."
Which friend haven't you
thanked recently?

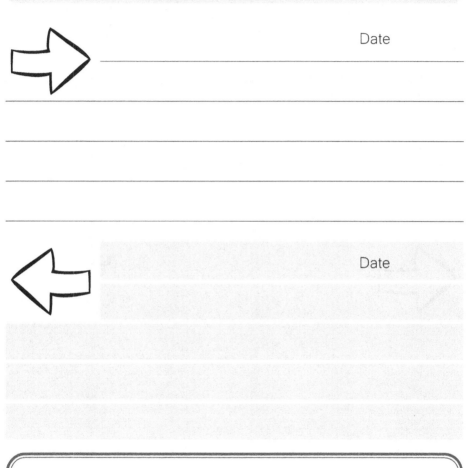

Date

Date

Free Space

MIND HIKE

QUESTION 90

When was the last time you were a "straight shooter"?

Date

Date

Free Space

MIND HIKE

QUESTION 91

Whose calls do you never answer on speaker phone?

Date
_____

Date

Free Space

MIND HIKE

QUESTION 92

What is your biggest regret?

Date

_____

_____

_____

_____

Date

Free Space

MIND HIKE

QUESTION 93

Who are you?

→
Date
_____

_____

_____

_____

←
Date

Free Space

MIND HIKE

Who is the most street smart person you know?

→ Date
_____

_____

_____

_____

_____

← Date

Bonus Question: **Book smart?**

QUESTION 95

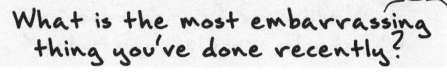

What is the most embarrassing thing you've done recently?

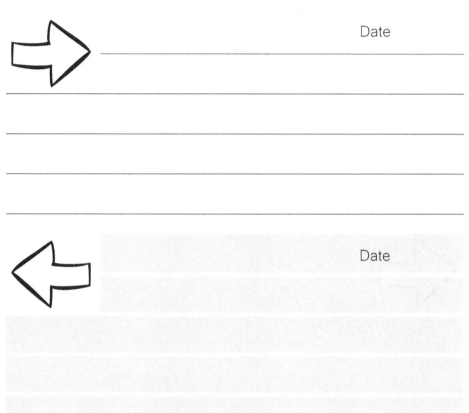

Date

Date

Free Space

QUESTION 96

Would your friends from high school recognize you today?

→ Date
_____

_____

_____

_____

← Date

Bonus Question: How have you changed?

MIND HIKE

QUESTION 97
How often do you really listen?

Date

Date

Free Space

MIND HIKE

QUESTION 98

What isn't working
in your life?

→   Date
_____
_____

_____

_____

←   Date

Free Space

MIND HIKE

What is your go-to outfit?

Date

Date

Free Space

QUESTION 100

When was the last time you had a mind-altering experience (chemically induced or otherwise)?

Date

Date

Free Space

MIND HIKE

QUESTION 101

What is one of your strengths that is also a weakness?

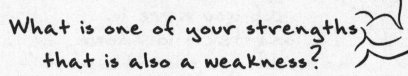

Date

_____

_____

_____

_____

Date

Free Space

MIND HIKE

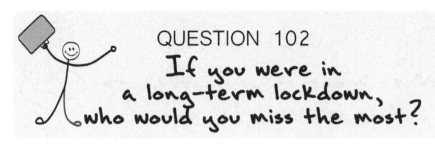

QUESTION 102
If you were in
a long-term lockdown,
who would you miss the most?

Date
_____

_____

_____

_____

Date

Bonus Question: What activity would you miss the most?

MIND HIKE

QUESTION 103

What have you put off doing?

Date

Date

Free Space

MIND HIKE

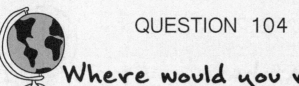

QUESTION 104

Where would you rather be right now?

Date

Date

Free Space

MIND HIKE

QUESTION 105

When was the last time you cried in front of someone else?

Date

Date

Bonus Question: By yourself?

QUESTION 106

When was the last time you were inconsistent?

Date
_____

Date

Free Space

MIND HIKE

QUESTION 107

"Things happen for a reason." Can you give one recent example?

Date
_____

_____

_____

_____

Date

Free Space

MIND HIKE

QUESTION 108

Did you spend more time on your needs or someone else's needs today?

Date
_____

_____

_____

_____

Date

Free Space

QUESTION 109

What's the last daring thing you did?

Date

Date

Free Space

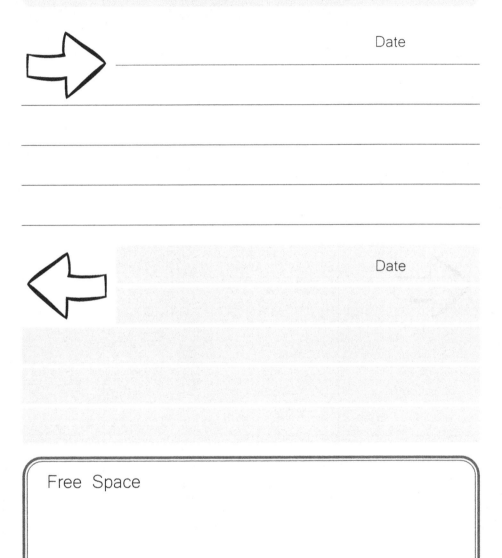

MIND HIKE

QUESTION 110

What do you really need today?

Date

_____

_____

_____

_____

Date

Bonus Question: **What do you not?**

MIND HIKE

What was the best job you ever had?

Date

Date

Bonus Question: **Worst job?**

QUESTION 112

What is your biggest impediment to happiness?

Date
_____

_____

_____

_____

_____

Date

Free Space

QUESTION 113

How well are you able to leave work behind when the work day ends?

Date

_____

Date

Free Space

QUESTION 114

What are you doing to keep up with the changes in the world?

→ Date _____

_____

_____

_____

← Date _____

Free Space

MIND HIKE

QUESTION 115

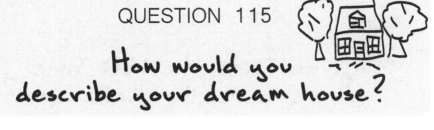

How would you describe your dream house?

Date
_____

Date

Bonus Question: **Who lives with you?**

When was the last time you were really challenged?

Date
_____

Date

Free Space

MIND HIKE

QUESTION 117

What's your most recent missed opportunity?

Date
_____

Date

Free Space

MIND HIKE

QUESTION 118

What are you neglecting right now?

Date
_____

_____

_____

_____

Date

Bonus Question: **Why?**

QUESTION 119

What time did you turn off technology last night?

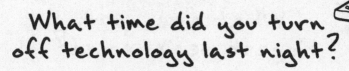

→ Date
_____

_____

_____

_____

← Date

Free Space

MIND HIKE

QUESTION 120

What are your biggest weaknesses?

Date
_____

_____

_____

_____

Date

Bonus Question: **How can you improve them?**

QUESTION 121

Which three people are most important to you right now?

→
Date
_____

_____

_____

_____

←
Date

Free Space

QUESTION 122

When was the last time
you were angry with someone?

Date

Date

Bonus Question: Why?

MIND HIKE

QUESTION 123

" "

What's your favorite quote?

→ Date
_____

_____

_____

_____

_____

← Date

Free Space

MIND HIKE

QUESTION 124

What failures have shaped who you are?

Date
_____

_____

_____

_____

_____

Date

Bonus Question: **What successes?**

QUESTION 125

Rank the following from most to least important: wealth, power, fame, satisfaction, work-life balance, improving the world.

→ Date
_____

_____

_____

_____

← Date

Free Space

MIND HIKE

What is your favorite thing in your house?

Date

Date

Bonus Question: Least favorite thing?

MIND HIKE

QUESTION 127

What changes need to be made in your life?

➡️ Date
_____

_____

_____

_____

_____

⬅️ Date

Bonus Question: What is preventing them?

MIND HIKE

QUESTION 128

When was the last time you made amends?

Date
_____

_____

_____

_____

_____

Date

Free Space

MIND HIKE

QUESTION 129

When was the last time you celebrated?

Date
_____

Date

Free Space

MIND HIKE

QUESTION 130

How much energy do you spend worrying about being liked by people?

Date

_____

Date

Bonus Question: **Respected?**

QUESTION 131

What is one thing you can do to handle stress better?

Date
_____

_____

_____

_____

Date

Free Space

MIND HIKE

QUESTION 132

What is your biggest fear?

Date
_____

_____

_____

_____

_____

Date

Free Space

MIND HIKE

QUESTION 133

Which family member do you have the least contact with?

Date
_____

_____

_____

_____

Date

Bonus Question: Why?

MIND HIKE

QUESTION 134

What is one thing you can change to be 10% happier?

Date
_____

Date

Free Space

MIND HIKE

QUESTION 135

How do you think your body is aging?

→ Date
_____

_____

_____

_____

_____

← Date

Free Space

MIND HIKE

QUESTION 136

What was the last swear word you used?

Date
_____

_____

_____

_____

_____

Date

Bonus Question: **Why did you say it?**

QUESTION 137

How many hours a day
do you spend sitting?

→ Date
_____

_____

_____

_____

_____

← Date

Free Space

MIND HIKE

QUESTION 138

When was the last time you were really shocked?

Date
_____

Date

Free Space

MIND HIKE

What are you suffering from right now?

Date
_____

_____

_____

_____

Date

"Suffering usually relates to wanting things to be different than the way they are." - Pema Chodron

MIND HIKE

QUESTION 140

How do you dress your part?

Date
_____

_____

_____

_____

_____

Date

Free Space

MIND HIKE

QUESTION 141

If you could vacation anywhere in the world for one month, where would it be?

Date

Date

Free Space

MIND HIKE

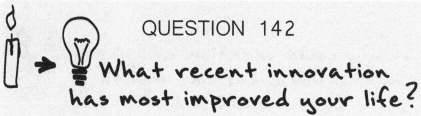

QUESTION 142

What recent innovation has most improved your life?

Date
_____

_____

_____

_____

_____

Date

Free Space

MIND HIKE

What was the last decision you struggled with?

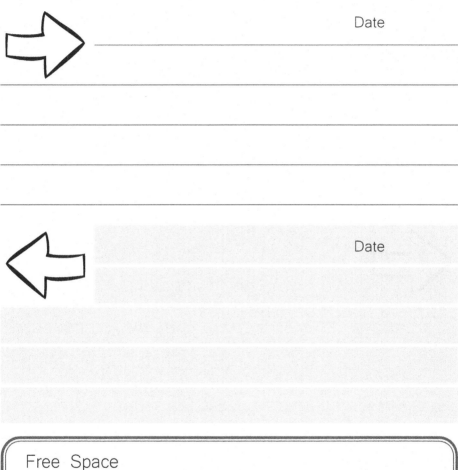

Date

Date

Free Space

MIND HIKE

QUESTION 144

How can you become better organized?

Date

_____

Date

Free Space

QUESTION 145

Would you rather have more money or more free time?

→ Date
_____

_____

_____

_____

← Date

Free Space

MIND HIKE

QUESTION 146

What TV show best describes your life?

Date

Date

Free Space

MIND HIKE

QUESTION 147

Who is your mentor?

→ Date
_____

_____

_____

_____

← Date

Bonus Question: If you could pick any mentor, who would you pick?

MIND HIKE

QUESTION 148

Whose calls do you usually ignore?

Date
_____

Date

Free Space

MIND HIKE

QUESTION 149

How old do you feel today?

Date
_____

Date

Free Space

QUESTION 150

Who is the most recent friend you made?

→ Date
_____

_____

_____

_____

← Date

Bonus Question: **How did you meet?**

MIND HIKE

QUESTION 151

When was the last time you felt spiritually connected?

Date

Date

Free Space

MIND HIKE

QUESTION 152

What could you cut out
of your budget with
no regrets?

→ Date
_____

_____

_____

_____

_____

← Date

Bonus Question: What can't you?

MIND HIKE

QUESTION 153

What do you want to be an expert in?

Date
_____

_____

_____

_____

Date

Bonus Question: What are you an expert in?

MIND HIKE

QUESTION 154

What is the best thing a former significant other would say about you?

Date
_____

_____

_____

_____

Date

Bonus Question: **Who was your worst significant other?**

MIND HIKE

QUESTION 155

How often did you think about money today?

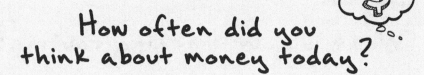

Date

Date

Free Space

MIND HIKE

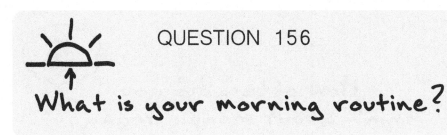

QUESTION 156

What is your morning routine?

Date

Date

Free Space

QUESTION 157

When was the last time you were hungover?

Date
_____

Date

Bonus Question: When were you the most hungover?

QUESTION 158

If you were to summarize your day in a song, which song would it be?

Date

Date

Free Space

MIND HIKE

QUESTION 159

If you had to prepare a resume today, whom would you list as references?

Date
_____

_____

_____

_____

Date

Bonus Question: Whom would you not list?

MIND HIKE

What is one thing you can change to be more efficient?

Date

Date

Free Space

MIND HIKE

QUESTION 161

If you had to live
in a different time period,
which would it be?

Date

Date

Free Space

MIND HIKE

QUESTION 162

Who was the last person to take advantage of you?

Date
_____

_____

_____

_____

_____

Date

Bonus Question: That you took advantage of?

What was the most inappropriate thing you've done recently?

Date

Date

Free Space

MIND HIKE

QUESTION 164

If you needed advice on a personal issue, which of your friends would you go to?

Date

Date

Free Space

MIND HIKE

QUESTION 165

Who sends the most annoying emails?

Date
_____

_____

_____

_____

_____

Date

Free Space

MIND HIKE

QUESTION 166

When do you feel most powerful?

Date
_____

_____

_____

_____

_____

Date

Free Space

What was the last project you avoided?

Date
_____

_____

_____

_____

_____

Date

Free Space

MIND HIKE

QUESTION 168

Which friend/family member would go farthest on a reality show?

Date

Date

Bonus Question: In a zombie apocalypse?

MIND HIKE

QUESTION 169

What do you do when you need to escape?

Date

Date

Free Space

When was the last time
you had to apologize?

Date
_____

_____

_____

_____

_____

Date

Bonus Question: Was it genuine?

MIND HIKE

QUESTION 171

Whom do you trust the most?

Date
_____

Date

Bonus Question: **The least?**

QUESTION 172

How often do you check social media?

→ Date
_____

_____

_____

_____

_____

← Date

Free Space

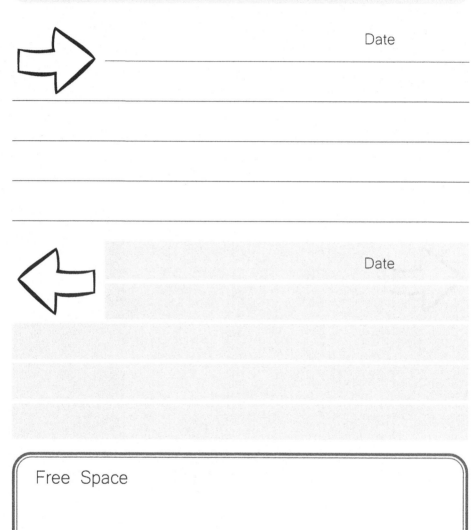

MIND HIKE

QUESTION 173

When was the last time you "phoned it in"?

→ Date
_____

_____

_____

_____

← Date

Bonus Question: Went above and beyond?

MIND HIKE

QUESTION 174

If you lost everything, who would still be standing next to you?

Date

Date

Bonus Question: **Who would leave?**

MIND HIKE

QUESTION 175

What has best prepared you for life?

Date

Date

Bonus Question: What additional training could help you?

MIND HIKE

"Even if you are on the right track, you'll get run over if you just sit there." Will Rogers

GUIDEPOST #2: Halfway! (Halfway through the first leg of the journey, or halfway through the final leg or whichever point you find yourself on your own journey). Great job. Maybe you didn't think you would make it this far? Or, once again, maybe you skipped ahead and just found yourself at Guidepost #2? That's cool too.

TASK: Laughter is the best medicine. Draw something below that will literally make you LOL.

....
....
....
....
....
....
....
....
....

MIND HIKE

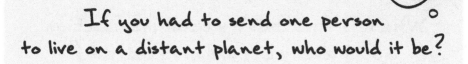

QUESTION 176

If you had to send one person to live on a distant planet, who would it be?

Date

Date

Free Space

MIND HIKE

What is the best recommendation
you have recently received?

Date

Date

Free Space

MIND HIKE

QUESTION 178

How are you best able
to express yourself?

Date

Date

Free Space

MIND HIKE

QUESTION 179

Who challenges you to be a better person?

Date
_____

_____

_____

_____

_____

Date

Bonus Question: **Who do you challenge to be a better person?**

QUESTION 180

If you could block one phone number without consequence, whose would it be?

Date
_____

_____

_____

_____

Date

Bonus Question: Who is currently blocked on your phone?

MIND HIKE

QUESTION 181

What was the last risk that you took?

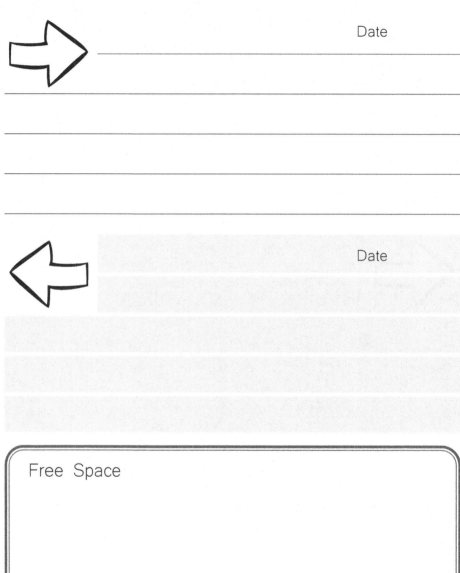

Date

_____

_____

_____

_____

Date

Free Space

MIND HIKE

If you could read anyone's
email, whose would it be?

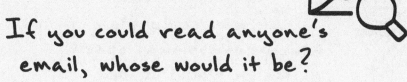

Date

Date

Free Space

MIND HIKE

QUESTION 183

If you could play
any professional sport,
which would it be?

Date
_____

_____

_____

_____

_____

Date

Bonus Question: **Why?**

QUESTION 184

What was the last nice thing that you did?

Date
_____

_____

_____

_____

_____

Date

Bonus Question: **Mean thing?**

MIND HIKE

What advice do you have for your 18 year old self?

Date
_____

Date

Bonus Question: 8 year old self?

MIND HIKE

QUESTION 186

If you had one year to live, how would you spend it?

Date

Date

Bonus Question: 10 years?

MIND HIKE

If you were to start a blog or a podcast, what would the topic be?

Date
_____

_____

_____

_____

Date

Free Space

MIND HIKE

QUESTION 188

When was the last time you worried about your finances?

→ Date
_____

_____

_____

_____

← Date

Free Space

QUESTION 189

What was the last picture that you drew?

➡️ _____ Date

_____

_____

_____

_____

⬅️ Date

Free Space

QUESTION 190

What was the last
impractical proposal
that you had to deal with?

Date

Date

Free Space

When was the last time
you felt like the third wheel?

Date

Date

Free Space

MIND HIKE

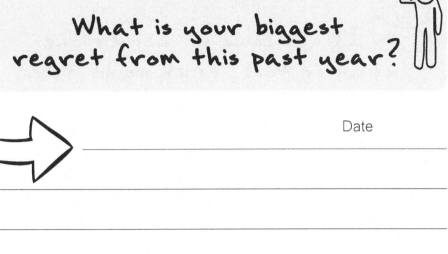

QUESTION 192

What is your biggest regret from this past year?

Date

Date

Free Space

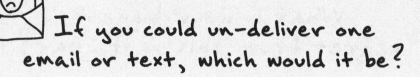

QUESTION 193

If you could un-deliver one email or text, which would it be?

Date
_____

_____

_____

_____

Date
_____

_____

_____

_____

Free Space

MIND HIKE

QUESTION 194

How well are your body and soul aligned?

Date

Date

Free Space

MIND HIKE

QUESTION 195

What was the last thoughtful present you gave?

Date
_____

Date

Bonus Question: **Received?**

MIND HIKE

How close are you to the
top rung of your ladder?

Date
_____

_____

_____

_____

Date

Free Space

MIND HIKE

QUESTION 197

Did you follow in your parents' footsteps or family members' footsteps?

Date
_____

_____

_____

_____

_____

Date

Bonus Question: Would you encourage a family member to follow in your footsteps?

MIND HIKE

QUESTION 198

What was the last thing you got up early for?

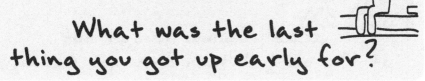

Date

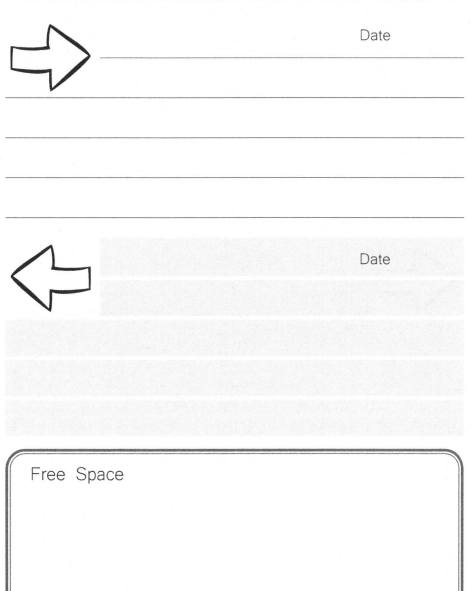

Date

Free Space

MIND HIKE

QUESTION 199

Lead, follow or get out
of the way. Which are you today?

Date

Date

Free Space

MIND HIKE

QUESTION 200

How would you rate your overall satisfaction level this year with your life (1-10)?

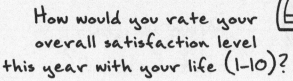

Date
_____

_____

_____

_____

Date

Free Space

MIND HIKE

QUESTION 201

Who is your best friend?

Date
_____

_____

_____

_____

_____

Date

Bonus Question: **Worst enemy?**

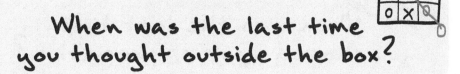

When was the last time you thought outside the box?

Date

_____

_____

_____

_____

Date

Free Space

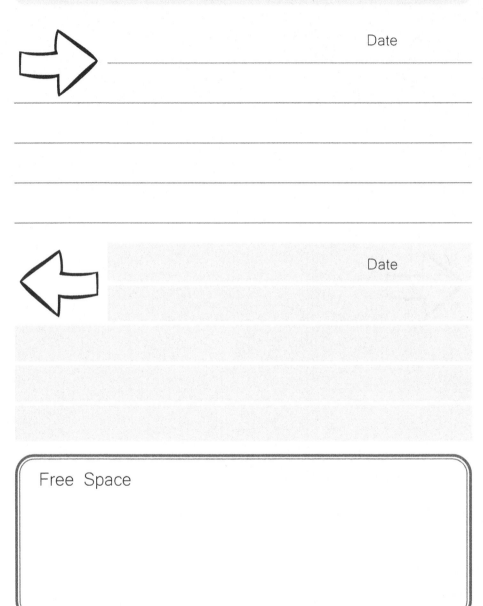

QUESTION 203

When was the last time you showed your appreciation?

Date

Date

Free Space

MIND HIKE

QUESTION 204

How much of your identity is tied up in what you do for a living?

Date
_____

_____

_____

_____

Date

Bonus Question: Your physical appearance?

MIND HIKE

QUESTION 205

When was the last time you tried to relive your childhood?

→

Date
_____

_____

_____

_____

_____

←

Date

Free Space

MIND HIKE

When was the last time you were out of it?

➡️ Date
_____

_____

_____

_____

_____

⬅️ Date

Free Space

MIND HIKE

QUESTION 207

If you had to marry a friend, whom would it be?

➡️ Date
_____

_____

_____

_____

⬅️ Date

Free Space

MIND HIKE

QUESTION 208

When was the last time you were afraid?

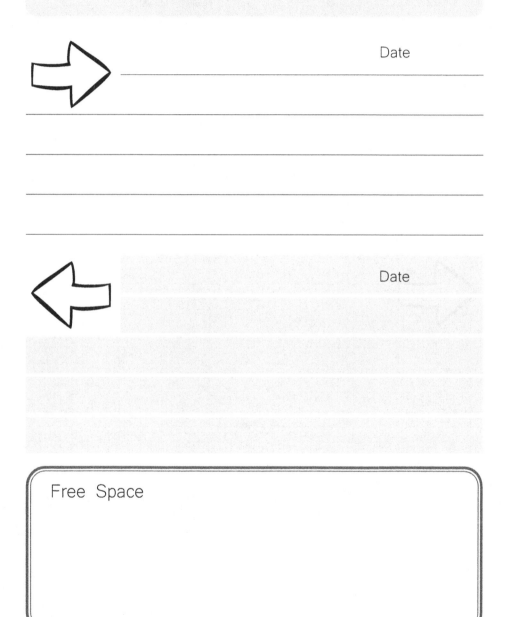

→ Date
_____

_____

_____

_____

← Date

Free Space

MIND HIKE

QUESTION 209

If you could start your
life all over again, what would
you do differently?

Date

Date

Free Space

MIND HIKE

QUESTION 210

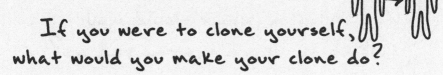

If you were to clone yourself, what would you make your clone do?

Date
_____

Date

Free Space

MIND HIKE

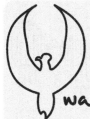

QUESTION 211

Who or what would you want to be reincarnated as?

Date
_____

_____

_____

_____

_____

Date

Free Space

MIND HIKE

QUESTION 212

Who is your "you have one phone call" contact?

Date

Date

Bonus Question: **When was the last time you called them?**

MIND HIKE

QUESTION 213

When was the last time you worked on personal growth?

Date
_____

_____

_____

_____

Date

Free Space

MIND HIKE

What is the biggest threat to your future?

Date
_____

_____

_____

_____

Date

Free Space

QUESTION 215

Who is the person you have the most difficulty spending time with?

→ Date

_____

_____

_____

_____

_____

← Date

Free Space

MIND HIKE

What gets you excited?

Date
_____

_____

_____

_____

Date

Bonus Question: **What brings you down?**

QUESTION 217

What problem seems impossible to solve?

→

Date
_____

_____

_____

_____

_____

←

Date

Free Space

MIND HIKE

QUESTION 218

What was the last purchase you made that you were excited about?

Date

Date

Bonus Question: **That you regretted?**

MIND HIKE

QUESTION 219

When was the last time you were late?

→ Date
_____

_____

_____

_____

_____

← Date

Bonus Question: **Why?**

MIND HIKE

QUESTION 220

Who was the last person you opened up to?

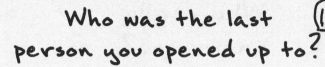

Date

Date

Free Space

QUESTION 221

Who really knows you?

→ _____ Date

_____

_____

_____

_____

 Date

Bonus Question: Who do you really know?

MIND HIKE

QUESTION 222

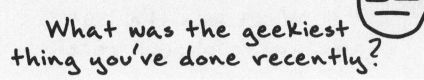

What was the geekiest thing you've done recently?

Date
_____

Date

Bonus Question: **Coolest?**

MIND HIKE

What was the last game you've played recently?

Date

Date

Free Space

MIND HIKE

QUESTION 224

"Trust but verify" - probably somebody famous and also Mike. In what ways do you buy into this idea?

Date
_____

Date

Bonus Question: **When was the last time someone broke your trust?**

MIND HIKE

QUESTION 225

What is one thing you could improve on?

→ Date
_____

_____

_____

_____

← Date

Free Space

MIND HIKE

QUESTION 226

What accomplishment are you most proud of?

Date

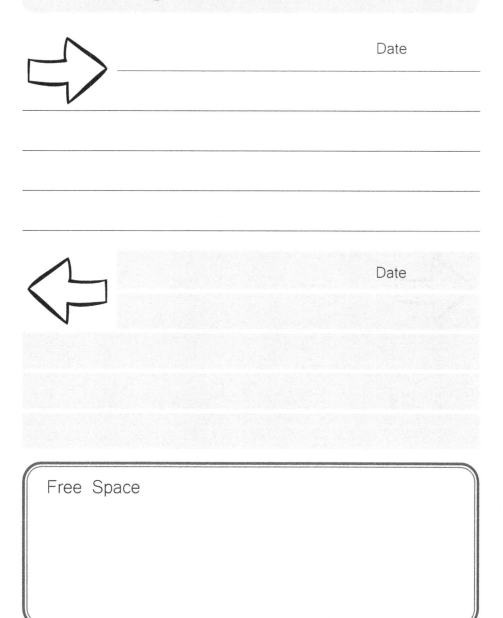

Date

Free Space

QUESTION 227

What inspires you?

Date _____

_____

_____

_____

_____

Date _____

Free Space

QUESTION 228

"Keep your friends close and your enemies closer." Which enemies are you keeping closer?

Date
_____

_____

_____

_____

Date

Free Space

How much value do you place on recognition or awards?

Date

_____

Date

Bonus Question: What award do you want to win?

MIND HIKE

QUESTION 230

When was the last time you
succeeded in cutting your expenses?

Date

Date

Free Space

MIND HIKE

QUESTION 231

When was the last time you exercised?

Date
_____

_____

_____

_____

Date

Free Space

QUESTION 232

Which of your relationships have grown the most over the past year?

Date

Date

Bonus Question: **Shrunk the most?**

MIND HIKE

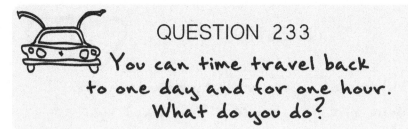

QUESTION 233
You can time travel back
to one day and for one hour.
What do you do?

Date
_____

_____

_____

_____

Date

Bonus Question: What is your favorite
time travel movie?

QUESTION 234

What's your next adventure?

Date

_____

_____

_____

_____

_____

Date

Free Space

MIND HIKE

$$$ QUESTION 235

If you received a $100,000 gift, how would you spend it?

Date
_____

Date

Free Space

MIND HIKE

QUESTION 236

What has most opened up your world?

Date
_____

_____

_____

_____

Date

Free Space

MIND HIKE

QUESTION 237

What is your most important core value?

→ Date
_____

_____

_____

_____

_____

← Date

Free Space

MIND HIKE

QUESTION 238

What is your biggest vice?

Date

Date

Free Space

QUESTION 239

How are you at setting boundaries?

Date

Date

Free Space

MIND HIKE

QUESTION 240

When was the last time
you got together
with an old friend?

Date

Date

Free Space

MIND HIKE

QUESTION 241

When was the last time your health impacted your day?

Date

Date

Free Space

MIND HIKE

What was the best decision you made this week?

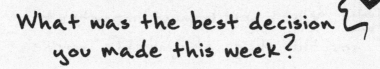

Date

Date

Bonus Question: **This year?**

MIND HIKE

QUESTION 243

What skill is most important for this stage of your life journey?

Date
_____

_____

_____

_____

_____

Date

Free Space

MIND HIKE

QUESTION 244

How strong is your inner circle?

Date

Date

Bonus Question: **Who is in your inner circle?**

QUESTION 245

There's a fire at your home. What is the one thing you grab on your way out?

Date

Date

Tip: It can't be a person or a pet.

MIND HIKE

QUESTION 246

When was the last time you stepped out of your comfort zone?

Date

Date

Free Space

MIND HIKE

QUESTION 247

What are you most looking forward to?

Date
_____

_____

_____

_____

_____

Date
_____

Bonus Question: **Least looking forward to?**

MIND HIKE

QUESTION 248

What is one small thing you can change to make your day better?

Date
_____

Date

Free Space

MIND HIKE

QUESTION 249

Why did you choose your career?

→ _____ Date
_____
_____
_____
_____

← _____ Date

Bonus Question: **Why do you stay in it?**

MIND HIKE

QUESTION 250

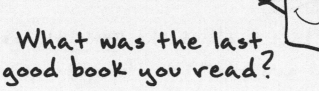

What was the last good book you read?

Date
_____

_____

_____

_____

_____

Date

Bonus Question: **Bad book?**

MIND HIKE

QUESTION 251

"Life is about the little things."
What are the little things in your life?

Date
_____

_____

_____

_____

_____

Date

Free Space

MIND HIKE

QUESTION 252

What's your most destructive habit?

→ Date
_____

_____

_____

_____

← Date

Bonus Question: **Most productive?**

QUESTION 253

What was the last goal that you set for yourself?

Date
_____

_____

_____

_____

_____

Date

Bonus Question: Did you accomplish it? Why/why not?

Are you good at budgeting?

Date
_____

_____

_____

_____

_____

Date

Bonus Question: How can you be better?

MIND HIKE

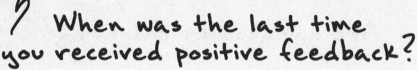

When was the last time
you received positive feedback?

Date
_____

_____

_____

_____

Date

Free Space

MIND HIKE

QUESTION 256

Work+Family+Fun = 100%.
What does your equation look like?

Date
_____

Date

Free Space

MIND HIKE

QUESTION 257

When was the last time you were disappointed?

Date
_____

Date

Free Space

MIND HIKE

QUESTION 258

What medicine do you take regularly?

→ Date
_____

_____

_____

_____

_____

← Date

Free Space

MIND HIKE

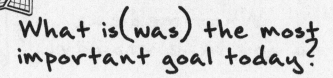

QUESTION 259

What is (was) the most important goal today?

Date

Date

Free Space

MIND HIKE

QUESTION 260

Where will your next vacation be?

→ Date
_____

_____

_____

_____

← Date

Bonus Question: **Where was your last?**

MIND HIKE

QUESTION 261

What's the best conversation you've had recently?

→ Date _____

_____
_____
_____
_____

← Date _____

Bonus Question: **Worst?**

MIND HIKE

QUESTION 262

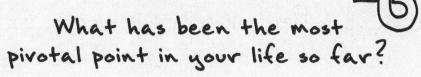

What has been the most pivotal point in your life so far?

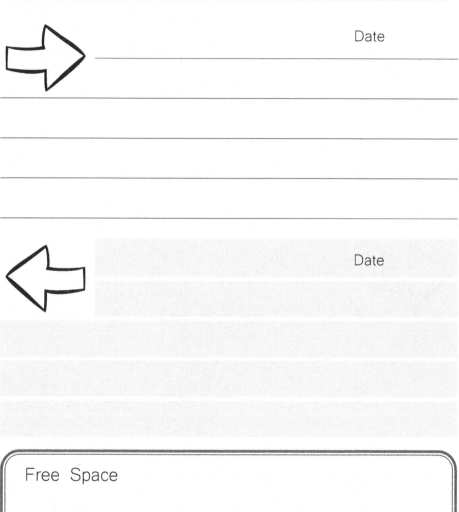

Date

_____

_____

_____

_____

Date

Free Space

MIND HIKE

QUESTION 263

How supportive is your significant other of your life choices?

Date
_____

_____

_____

_____

Date

Tip: (If no significant other — substitute best friend or parents.)

MIND HIKE

What are your guilty pleasures?

Date

Date

Free Space

MIND HIKE

QUESTION 265

What would you do
if you were given a one-month
sabbatical from work?

Date
_____

_____

_____

_____

_____

Date

Bonus Question: **One year?**

MIND HIKE

QUESTION 266

What's your current obsession?

Date

Date

Free Space

MIND HIKE

QUESTION 267

How do you recover from a bad day?

Date
_____

_____

_____

_____

_____

Date

Bonus Question: **What caused your most recent bad day?**

QUESTION 268

How will you be different in 5 years?

Date
_____

_____

_____

_____

Date

Bonus Question: **What won't ever change?**

MIND HIKE

QUESTION 269

Where is your happy place?

Date
_____

_____

_____

_____

Date

Free Space

QUESTION 270

How long do you plan to continue at your current job (or if you're not working now, do you plan to find a job in the future)?

⟹ _____ Date

_____

_____

_____

_____

⟸ _____ Date

Bonus Question: **Where will you go next?**

QUESTION 271

When was the last time you compared yourself to someone else?

→ Date
_____

_____

_____

_____

_____

← Date

Free Space

MIND HIKE

QUESTION 272

Who did you spend the
most time with today?

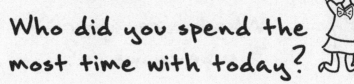

Date
_____

Date

Free Space

MIND HIKE

QUESTION 273

What are your 3 superpowers?

→   Date

←   Date

Free Space

MIND HIKE

QUESTION 274

What aspect of your life are you most proud of?

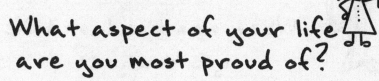

Date

Date

Bonus Question: **Least proud?**

MIND HIKE

QUESTION 275

When was the last time
you prayed?

Date
_____

_____

_____

_____

Date

Free Space

MIND HIKE

"Believe you can and you're halfway there." — President Theodore Roosevelt

GUIDEPOST #3: You've made it so far! Look at you, setting a goal and working so hard to meet it. You've made so much progress. You got this, dude. Keep it up.

Let's take a look behind us to appreciate how far you have come on this journey.

TASK: If this is the first leg of the journey, go back and highlight/star/asterisk 5 questions that you think will change the most when you answer them a second time. If this is the second leg of the journey, go back and highlight/star/asterisk 5 questions that changed the most when you answered them a second time.

QUESTION 276

What did you want to be when you grew up?

Date
_____

_____

_____

_____

Date

Bonus Question: **What do you want to be now?**

MIND HIKE

How can you be more intentional about your goals?

Date
_____

_____

_____

_____

Date

Free Space

MIND HIKE

QUESTION 278

Who was the last friend you lost?

Date
_____

_____

_____

_____

_____

Date

Bonus Question: **Why did you lose them?**

QUESTION 279

What is one thing you are grateful for?

→ Date
_____

_____

_____

_____

← Date

Free Space

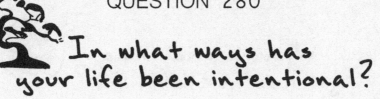

QUESTION 280

In what ways has your life been intentional?

→ Date
_____

_____

_____

_____

← Date

Bonus Question: Been based on the whims of fate?

QUESTION 281

When you woke up this morning,
how did you feel about starting your day?

→ Date
_____

_____

_____

_____

← Date

Free Space

MIND HIKE

QUESTION 282

What was the last funeral you attended?

Date

Date

Free Space

MIND HIKE

QUESTION 283

How is this year better than last year?

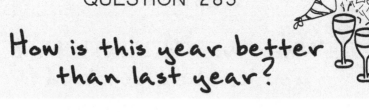

Date

Date

Bonus Question: **Worse?**

MIND HIKE

QUESTION 284

When was the last time you laughed out loud?

Date

Date

Free Space

When was the last time everything seemed to click into place?

Date
_____

Date

Free Space

MIND HIKE

QUESTION 286

What was the last movie you watched?

Date
_____

_____

_____

_____

Date

Free Space

What have you done to create happiness today?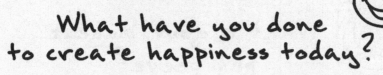

Date
_____

Date

"Happiness is created, not found" - Mike and the Internet

What is your biggest pet peeve?

Date

Date

Free Space

MIND HIKE

Who was the last person
you forgot having met before?

Date
_____

_____

_____

_____

Date

Bonus Question: Who was the last
person to forget your name?

MIND HIKE

QUESTION 290

What do you like most about yourself today?

Date
_____

_____

_____

_____

_____

Date

Free Space

MIND HIKE

QUESTION 291

If you had to start a business, what would it be?

Date

⇒

⇐ Date

Free Space

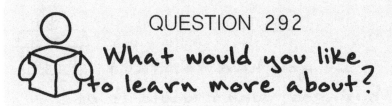

QUESTION 292

What would you like to learn more about?

Date
_____

_____

_____

_____

Date

Bonus Question: **What is the first step you would take?**

QUESTION 293

What was the last great meal you had?

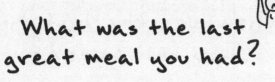

Date

Date

Free Space

MIND HIKE

QUESTION 294
When was the last time you felt jaded?

Date
_____

Date

Tip: Jaded means tired, bored or lacking enthusiasm, typically after having had too much of something.

QUESTION 295

How have you made your life pandemic proof?

Date

Date

Free Space

MIND HIKE

QUESTION 296

Who was the last new person you met?

Date
_____

_____

_____

_____

Date

Free Space

QUESTION 297

If you could re-live one day, which one would it be?

Date

Date

Free Space

MIND HIKE

QUESTION 298

When was the last time you ruined someone's day?

Date
_____

Date

Free Space

MIND HIKE

QUESTION 299

When was the last time someone doubted you?

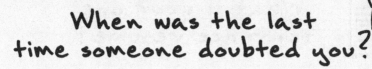

Date
_____

_____

_____

_____

_____

Date

Free Space

MIND HIKE

QUESTION 300

What is your one sentence resume?

Date

_____

_____

_____

_____

Date

Bonus Question: How old is your last resume?

MIND HIKE

QUESTION 301

What weighs most heavy on your heart right now?

Date

Date

Free Space

QUESTION 302

If you quit your job today, who would hire you tomorrow?

Date

_____

Date

Free Space

MIND HIKE

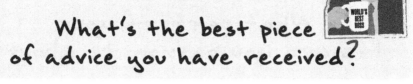

What's the best piece of advice you have received?

Date
_____

_____

_____

_____

Date

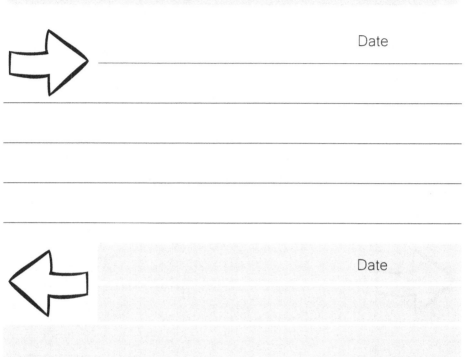

"Don't be an idiot. Changed my life." -Dwight K. Schrute

MIND HIKE

QUESTION 304

What parts of your life are you passionate about?

Date
_____

_____

_____

_____

_____

Date

Free Space

MIND HIKE

QUESTION 305

When was the last time you made someone laugh?

Date

Date

Free Space

MIND HIKE

What was the last decision that you regretted?

Date

_____

_____

_____

_____

Date

Free Space

MIND HIKE

What was the last phone call that you ignored?

Date

_____

_____

_____

_____

Date

Free Space

MIND HIKE

When was the last time you felt deflated?

Date
_____

_____

_____

_____

_____

Date

Bonus Question: **What happened?**

QUESTION 309

Do you have an unspoken rule?

Date

Date

Free Space

QUESTION 310

How happy are you with your income this year?

→ Date
_____

_____

_____

_____

_____

← Date

Free Space

MIND HIKE

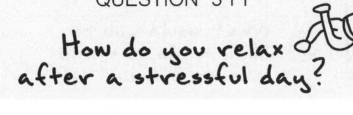

How do you relax after a stressful day?

Date

Date

Free Space

MIND HIKE

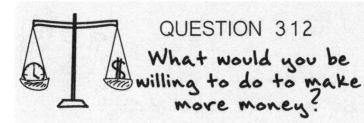

QUESTION 312

What would you be willing to do to make more money?

Date
_____

_____

_____

_____

Date

Bonus Question: **Work an extra two hours a day? Move to another city?**

MIND HIKE

QUESTION 313

What is your biggest secret?

Date

————————————————

Date

Free Space

MIND HIKE

QUESTION 314

What was your
last failed relationship?

Date

Date

Free Space

QUESTION 315

When did you last break something or someone?

Date

Date

Free Space

QUESTION 316

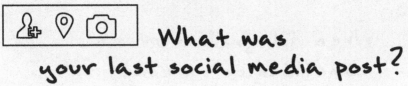 What was
your last social media post?

Date
_____

_____

_____

_____

Date

Free Space

QUESTION 317

Who are your idols?

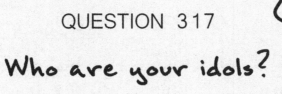

Date

Date

Free Space

MIND HIKE

QUESTION 318

What was the biggest
challenge you have faced this year?

Date
_____

_____

_____

_____

Date

Bonus Question: How did you handle it?

QUESTION 319

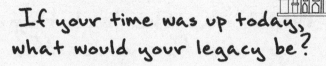

If your time was up today, what would your legacy be?

Date

Date

Free Space

QUESTION 320

What was the last thing you did for yourself?

Date

Date

Free Space

MIND HIKE

QUESTION 321

What book do you like to give as a present?

Date

Date

Free Space

MIND HIKE

QUESTION 322

What might seem minor to other people, but is a big deal to you?

Date

Date

Free Space

QUESTION 323

What was the last
lie you told?

Date

Date

Free Space

MIND HIKE

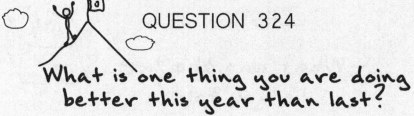

QUESTION 324

What is one thing you are doing better this year than last?

Date

Date

Free Space

Who is the one that got away?

Date
_____

_____

_____

_____

Date

Bonus Question: **Why?**

MIND HIKE

QUESTION 326

Where do you see yourself in 10 years?

Date
_____

_____

_____

_____

Date

Free Space

MIND HIKE

QUESTION 327

What was the last decision that you made on principle?

Date

Date

Free Space

MIND HIKE

What loss has had the most significant impact on your life?

Date
_____

_____

_____

_____

Date

Free Space

MIND HIKE

QUESTION 329

Are you on the right path?

Date

Date

Bonus Question: **Why/why not?**

MIND HIKE

QUESTION 330

What is the single best thing about you?

Date

Date

Free Space

MIND HIKE

QUESTION 331
How many days off
(real days off)
did you take last year?

Date
_____

_____

_____

_____

Date
_____

_____

_____

_____

Free Space

MIND HIKE

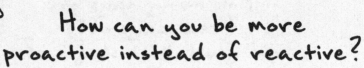

How can you be more proactive instead of reactive?

→ Date
_____

_____

_____

_____

_____

← Date

Free Space

QUESTION 333

"What would you do if you weren't afraid?" - Sheryl Sandberg

Date

Date

Free Space

MIND HIKE

QUESTION 334

What cliched line would you use to describe this last year?

→   Date
_____

_____

_____

_____

←   Date

Free Space

MIND HIKE

QUESTION 335

Who is your biggest adversary?

→ _____ Date

_____

_____

_____

_____

← _____ Date

Free Space

MIND HIKE

QUESTION 336

What was the last problem that you fixed with money?

Date
_____

_____

_____

_____

Date

"Any problem that can be fixed with money isn't the worst problem to have." -Elissa's Dad

MIND HIKE

What did you learn from your last failure?

Date
_____

_____

_____

_____

Date

Free Space

MIND HIKE

QUESTION 338

If your significant other left you tomorrow, what would you do?

Date
_____

_____

_____

_____

_____

Date

If you don't have a significant other, why?

MIND HIKE

QUESTION 339

When was the last time you grew?

Date

Date

Free Space

QUESTION 340

When was the last time you had to speak up about an uncomfortable problem?

Date

_____

_____

_____

_____

Date

Free Space

MIND HIKE

QUESTION 341

Who was the last person you asked for a favor?

Date
_____

Date

Bonus Question: **Was it granted?**

MIND HIKE

QUESTION 342

When was the last time you moved for work?

→ Date
_____

_____

_____

_____

_____

← Date

Bonus Question: **For love?**

MIND HIKE

QUESTION 343

How well are you keeping up with the times?

→ Date
_____

_____

_____

_____

← Date

Free Space

MIND HIKE

QUESTION 344

When was the last time you were brave?

Date
_____

Date

Free Space

MIND HIKE

QUESTION 345

What would be at the top of your do-not-do-list these days?

Date

Date

Free Space

MIND HIKE

QUESTION 346

What was the last question that you couldn't answer?

→ Date
_____

_____

_____

_____

← Date

Free Space

MIND HIKE

QUESTION 347

When was the last time you had to have the last word?

Date

Date

Free Space

MIND HIKE

QUESTION 348

When was the last time you were physically intimate with someone?

Date
_____

_____

_____

_____

Date

Free Space

MIND HIKE

QUESTION 349

When was the last time you swallowed your pride?

Date
_____

Date

Free Space

MIND HIKE

QUESTION 350

What was the last
review you gave?

→ Date
_____

_____

_____

_____

← Date

Free Space

QUESTION 351

When were you last surprised?

→ Date
_____

_____

_____

_____

← Date

Free Space

MIND HIKE

QUESTION 352

When was the last time you gave an excuse?

→   Date

_____

_____

_____

_____

←   Date

Free Space

QUESTION 353

When was the last time you were impatient?

Date

Date

Free Space

MIND HIKE

QUESTION 354

What is your perfect day?

Date

_____

_____

_____

_____

_____

Date

Bonus Question: **When was the last time you had a glorious day?**

MIND HIKE

QUESTION 355

How well do your pants fit today?

Date

Date

Free Space

QUESTION 356

When was the last time you really enjoyed the present?

Date
_____

_____

_____

_____

_____

Date

"[man] is so anxious about the future that he does not enjoy the present." - Dalai Lama

MIND HIKE

QUESTION 357

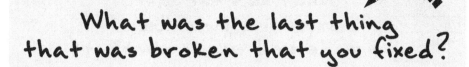

What was the last thing that was broken that you fixed?

Date
_____

_____

_____

_____

Date

Bonus Question: **That you haven't fixed?**

MIND HIKE

QUESTION 358

What was the last expensive purchase you made and was it worth it?

Date
_____

_____

_____

_____

_____

Date

"This just cost $100 for us to go here for the day, so you'd better have fun." - David's dad outside of Disney World to young David.

MIND HIKE

QUESTION 359

How difficult has it been to keep going on this journey?

Date
_____

_____

_____

_____

Date

Free Space

MIND HIKE

QUESTION 360

What is your favorite inside joke?

Date
_____

_____

_____

_____

Date
_____

Free Space

MIND HIKE

QUESTION 361

"You learn something
new every day."
What have you learned today?

Date

Date

Free Space

MIND HIKE

QUESTION 362

The average human lifespan
is approximately 28,725.5 days.
How are you making this day count?

Date

Date

Free Space

MIND HIKE

QUESTION 363

What are three things
that you are grateful
for in your life?

Date

Date

Free Space

MIND HIKE

QUESTION 364

What is your favorite snack?

Date
_____

_____

_____

_____

_____

Date

Free Space

QUESTION 365
[FILL IN THE BLANK.
What question do you
want to answer today?]

Date

Date

Free Space

MIND HIKE

"Sometimes the questions are complicated and the answers are simple." — Dr. Seuss

GUIDEPOST #4: You made it! We're happy to see you here. If you've made it all the way through your 365 questions (or through them twice), you've been working hard, and we salute you. Enjoy the view!

Whether this is the first leg or the final leg of your Mind Hike journey, we encourage you to spend a little time reflecting on yourself. If we weren't so cheap, we might have included a neat little mirror on this page. But instead we are asking you to do the hard work.

TASK: Create a self-portrait of how you see yourself today (below). You can use words or a collage or a paint brush or your favorite crayon.

....

....

....

....

....

....

Great Job. You have completed the first half of your Mind Hike journey. Now turn around and start again at Question 1.

You made it! You have completed your Mind Hike journey. We hope you enjoyed it!

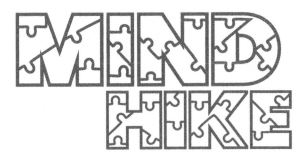